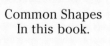

Images

Most images in this book are from clip art books by Dover Publica[tion] Stemmer House. They are copyright free and available to the public. You have per[mission to] use images in a craft application, provided you do not use more than ten images [from a] Dover book in any one project. For any other commercial purpose, you should con[tact them]. Other images were either hand-drawn or are now in the general domain because the copyright has expired.

First you need a photocopy. Different copy machines will produce different shades of Black or even Indigo Blue, but they all are toner based. Copies made with a digital printer or digital copier will not transfer to clay. The projects in this book were produced with a Canon personal copier.

The image should be sized appropriately and have ample space around the edges to avoid edge marks on clay. The image itself should be crisp Black and White. You can set the contrast level to high or experiment with different settings such as photo. Try to get the clearest contrast. Gray will not transfer in most cases. Line or pen and ink drawings are excellent. I have not noticed a difference in papers.

Transferring Images

Condition the clay and roll it into a flat sheet. The thickness will depend on how you are using the clay and how many layers you may add. The clay must be clean. Do not handle the clay, as oil from your hands may prevent the toner from transferring. Place the copy, toner side down, on one edge and smooth it onto the clay without trapping air. Burnish the paper with a bone folder or the back of a spoon to get an even seal and to eliminate any gaps where the paper may not touch the clay. Pressure on the edge of the paper will make an indentation in the clay, so you need to be aware of the space around the image, too. Allow the transfer to set.

Common Shapes
In this book.

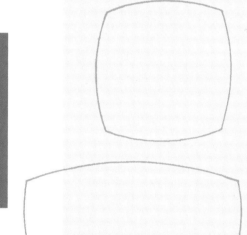

Timing

The amount of time it takes the toner to transfer depends on the clay brand, color, toner and room temperature. Do not attempt to transfer images in a cold environment. Generally the clay will transfer in one hour for Fimo to three hours for Premo. If you try to pull the paper up, you may find that it sticks to the clay. The transfer is not complete until the paper removes easily. You can speed this process by lightly coating the paper with alcohol. This helps to remove the toner. But do not oversaturate the paper, as the toner can actually melt and become smeared. A tip from Syndee Holt is to dampen the paper once, allow it to dry and then wet it again and remove the paper while it is still wet. This works quite well.

Removing Paper

You may notice that the ink appears to be different colors, Blue and Black, in different places. This is due to the concentration of ink and the amount that has actually been released. For best results, allow the piece to sit until the transfer is even. If the paper has not shifted, you can replace any portion that has been pulled off and continue to allow the transfer to set. Remove the paper in one even motion to avoid section pressure marks. You can also bake the paper on the clay and remove it afterward. If you remove it while it is still hot, it often will release quite easily. Sometimes the paper becomes so attached that you need to soak it off. Just place the baked clay in water and allow the paper to soak and shred. When the paper is rubbed off, the toner will remain adhered to the clay.

Good Things to Know

Basic Transfer Tips for Images

Image Transfers

Selecting an image is a personal choice, although you should be aware of the legal status of the use of that image. I recommend books by Dover Publications or a similar publisher that allow for copyright free use of designs. These may have restrictions but are the best source for images.

Reversing Image

When you place a photocopy face down on the clay, you will be transferring a 'mirror image'. In other words if your original portrait is facing right, the transfer will face left. When transferring writing, Asian characters or anything that must be transferred as a duplicate, you must first make a 'mirror image" copy which will reverse during the transfer process.

Toner Based Copier

Any picture can be transferred to polymer clay once it has been photocopied with a toner based copier. I have seen Blue toner to turn to Black after it has set on the uncured clay cured in sunlight. Polymer clays differ in brand formulations. Upgrades in clay and toner formulations may influence this phenomenon. The image will never change, but how we see the Blue or Black image due to chemical reactions to heat and light, may change the color.

Size the Image

Size the image as desired. Use a computer or photocopier to enlarge, shrink or add contrast to an image. Also set the printer to grayscale if you are sizing and printing your image on a computer. This will eliminate any other colors from interfering with the copy. Sometimes the copier machine does the work and will define the image as a photo type of drawing, but for the most part, crisp Black and White images transfer best. Expect to make a few tests before you discover the setting that gives the best results.

Before you begin, condition clay by folding and kneading it in your hands or use a pasta machine.

Tip: Polymer clay must be clean. Oils from your hands may prevent transfers from adhering. Once clay is prepared, try not to touch the clay or the photocopy with your fingers.

 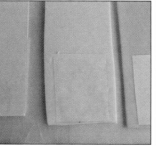 

1. Roll clay into flat sheet. Place transfer toner side down on clay. Burnish with a smooth tool such as a bone folder or back of a spoon to secure contact and eliminate air pockets. **2.** Your image should be large enough so the edge of the paper does not make a dent in the clay at the edge of the paper. **3.** Allow image to sit for one hour.

4. Lift corner of paper to test to see if transfer has taken. The image may transfer evenly, **5.** unevenly **6.** or not enough. If image has transferred to clay, lightly burnish transfer once more before you remove paper. Remove paper in one continuous pull. Do not touch exposed transfer as it will smear. Results and time will vary according to clay type, color, room temperature and sunlight. After a prolonged period, toner may bleed into the clay on certain brand formulations.

7. If the toner is difficult to transfer, you can dampen paper with alcohol to help release toner. **8.** Do not saturate paper, as it may smear the toner and the paper may tear. **9.** Allow to dry, dampen again and remove paper. You can also bake paper on clay and remove after baking. If paper is stuck after baking, soak piece in water and rub off paper as it shreds.

MATERIALS: Bride portrait transfer in 2 different sizes • Light color, White, Pearl or Translucent clay • Navy Pearl mix of ½ Blue Pearl and ½ Black Premo clay • Black Premo clay in thin sheets • *Limited Edition* clock and 2 script rubber stamps • Imprintz Gold pigment ink • Premo Shapelets Classic templates • Pin back • Concho • Craft knife • Super Sculpey slicer • Crafter's Pick Ultimate glue • Pres-On Goosh mounts

Portrait Pins

1. Condition and roll clay into flat sheets. Place transfer on light clay. Allow to sit, remove paper. 2. Bleeding occurs on certain clays. This project used Fimo Translucent.

3. Press one inked script stamp lightly on transferred images. 4. Stamp clock sparingly on image. Place square template over image in desired position. Cut out square with craft knife.

Often if you make more than one of something, you will develop subtle preferences on which to base future compositions. In this case, a comparison is made up of what type, Translucent, Pearl or White, clay is used and also the size and positioning of the portrait. You can also compare details such as how thick each layer is or the width of the borders. Ultimately, you'll have gifts for friends when you are finished!

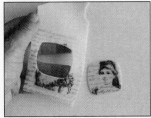
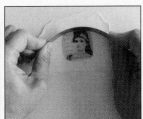

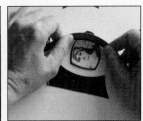

5. Pull blade through clay using template as a guide. 6. Move piece as needed to work comfortably. Remove cropped piece from sheet. 7. Using Translucent clay, bake it with a very thin layer of White. Translucent clay will reflect White. A dark background will gray Translucent. Bend slicer to cut curve. 8. Place cut image on a very thin Black sheet rolled at #6 setting. Bend blade and trim along edge, leaving a very thin border. 9. You can trim again after initial cut to even edges or get closer to border.

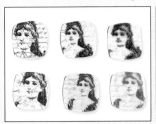

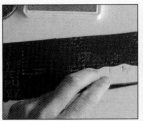

10. If you make several pieces, you can decide which design placement and size is your favorite. 11. Ink second script stamp and stamp strip of clay rolled at #5 setting. Do not touch ink or it will smear. Ink cures during baking. 12. You can also use a collage on the next layer. 13. Place prepared image on background. 14. Bend blade and cut a wide border for background. Trim again as needed.

15. Place work on another thin layer of Black. Use finger to edge work with Gold pigment. 16. Handle work gently and place it over a concho during baking for a slight curve. 17. Bake piece following manufacturer's instructions, let cool. Cut small square of clay. Coat lightly with Crafter's Pick glue to help baked clay adhere to unbaked clay. 18. Slip square over bar of pin back and attach pin to back of work. Bake again to cure added clay. 19. Attach piece to boxes or book covers by using flexible tacky mounts.

Modern Maid Picasso Doll

This modern maid is just the inspiration you need dancing on your file cabinet, jacket lapel or fridge.

MATERIALS: White Premo clay • Modern 'Picasso' transfer • *Limited Edition* blank doll rubber stamp • Craf-T Mini Metallics pigments • 18 gauge Copper wire for connecting parts • Magnet • Craft knife • Fine manicure sanding sponge • Cosmetic sponge or cotton swab • Craft drill • Wire cutters • Round-nose pliers • Super glue

 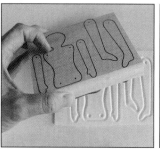  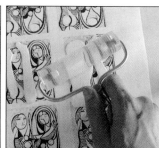

1. Condition and roll sheet of clay on #1 setting. Dampen clay with water. The water will act as a release for Premo clay. **2.** Press stamp into clay. **3.** Cut out parts with craft knife. **4.** Place clay strips on photocopy image. Place body parts on desired areas of photocopy. You will have a mirror image transfer. Roll image smooth, securing it to paper.

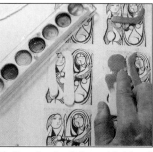 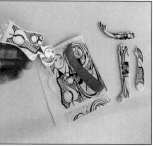  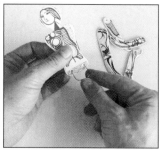

5. Coat back of clay with Metallic Gold pigment using finger, cosmetic sponge or cotton swab. **6.** Bake transfer directly on paper following manufacturer's instructions. Remove paper when baking is finished. **7.** Drill holes in individual parts. **8.** Cut 6" of wire and loop through front of body. Attach legs and arms from back.

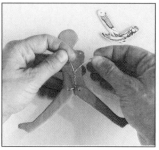   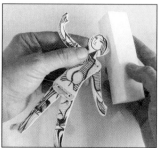

9. Twist wire together on back side. **10.** Twist until wire extends to midpoint of body. Loop 2 twisted wire sets from top and bottom and interlock. **11.** Cut ends to equal lengths and spiral. **12.** Sand edges with manicure sanding cube to remove any rough spots. Attach a magnet to back with super glue or make a wire loop hanger.

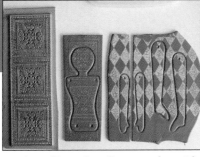

1. Condition and roll sheet of clay mix at #1 setting. Dampen clay with water. The water will act as a release for the clay. Press stamp into clay. **2.** Separate pieces and stamp with White ink. Ink will set when piece is baked.

3. Trim body parts with craft knife. **4.** Condition and roll sheet of White clay at #4 setting. Place transfers on clay. Bake. Remove paper. Trim pieces with straight or decorative scissors.

5. Glue baked torso and face to doll using Crafter's Pick. **6.** Bake doll. When clay is cooled, drill holes.

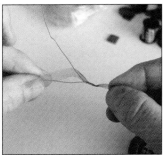 

7. Cut four 5" pieces of ribbon. Twist ribbon with wire to help thread it through doll. **8.** Connect arms and legs with ribbon.

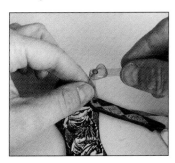

9. Tie beads for accents. Cut ribbon leaving ¾" tails at front and back.

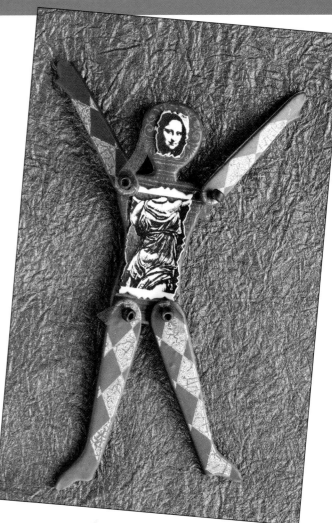

Clever moveable clay dolls swing arms and legs... dance, dance, dance all day long.

MATERIALS: Pearl Blue and Metallic Gold Premo clay mix (refer to color mixing on page 32) • White Premo clay • Mona Lisa face and torso transfers • *Limited Edition* blank doll rubber stamp • *Paper Inspirations* rubber stamps • Tsukineko White Brilliance ink • ¼" Gray sheer ribbon for connecting parts • 8 Iridescent Purple E beads • Magnet • Fiskars decorative scissors • Craft blade • Craft drill • Damp sponge • Fine manicure sanding sponge • Super glue • Crafter's Pick Ultimate glue

Triangle Ornament

This project is an extension of the basic concept of stacked layers. The difference is in the combination of shapes and the punches which create see-through layers.

MATERIALS: Pearl, Orange and Black Premo clay (refer to color mixing on page 32) • *Limited Edition* rubber stamps (face, script, Venetia column) • Imprintz Gold pigment ink • Inkredible heat set ink (Indian Rouge, Burnt Brass) • Kemper 1/8" and 3/32" nested square punches • Shapelets classic triangle template • Flexible blade • Craft knife • Pres-On Goosh Mounts

1. Condition and roll sheet of Pearl at #5 setting. Stamp collage grouping using dark inks for portrait and metallic inks for column and script. Place template to frame face and cut out. **2.** Using template as a guide, cut strip with same curves as triangle.

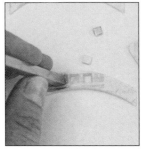

3. Assemble nested punch so outer tube and inner tube are flat squares on bottom, pull inner tube back. Punch clay with outer tube and slide inner tube down to remove punched square. Punch 3 holes in center of strip. Realign if crooked. **4.** Place face and strip on sheet of thin Black clay rolled at #6 setting. Bend blade and trim close to the shapes.

5. Place both pieces on sheet of Orange clay rolled at #5 setting. Leave space between pieces. **6.** Bend blade to trim layer. Place stacked piece on final sheet of Black and trim.

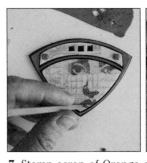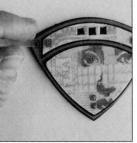

7. Stamp scrap of Orange clay with any design using Gold ink and punch a few tiny squares for accents. Place on corners of triangle. **8.** Optional: Punch 2 final squares through each corner and use holes to hang for pendant. Bake following manufacturer's instructions. Attach to a fabric purse with Goosh Mounts.

Map Panel

This map panel is an extension of the basic concept of stacked layers. The combination of shapes, punches and stamps create a fancinating and beautiful work of art.

MATERIALS: Pearl, Orange and Olive Green Premo clay (refer to color mixing on page 32) • Wrought iron frame with 3½" x 5" opening • *Limited Edition* rubber stamps (face, script, Venetia column) • Imprintz Gold pigment ink • Inkredible heat set ink (Indian Rouge, Burnt Brass) • 3½" x 5" piece of map print paper • Kemper ⅛" and ³⁄₃₂" nested square punches • Shapelets classic rectangle template • Flexible blade • Craft knife • Crafter's Pick Ultimate glue

INSTRUCTIONS: Follow instructions for triangle ornament but use rectangle template and refer to photo. The goal is to add 2 separate pieces that relate to each other in a pleasing composition.

1. Make bottom piece by stamping script stamp on Pearl and cutting shape that repeats shapes in top design. **2.** Frame shape with layer of Olive Green. Punch tiny squares of Pearl and Gold inked clay. Place squares on Olive Green clay and punch larger square around smaller squares.

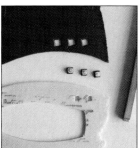 

3. Pull squares from clay sheet. **4.** Set square accents on script.

5. Bake clay pieces following manufacturer's instructions. **6.** Glue map print paper on glass, insert in frame and glue clay pieces on paper.

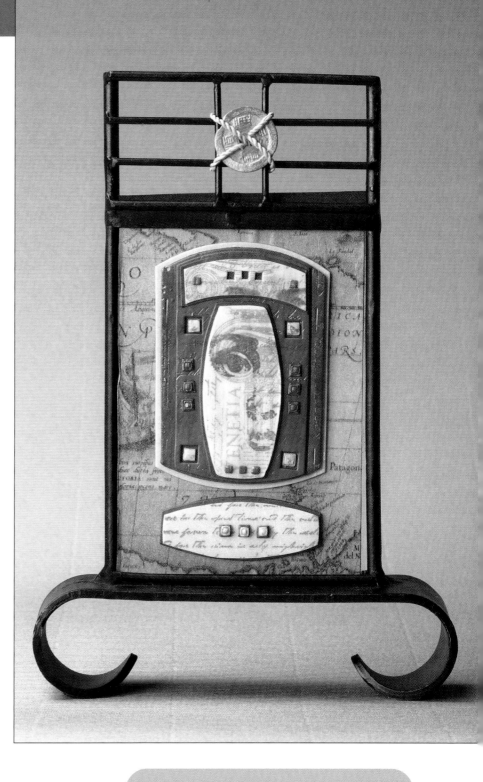

Tips

- Stamp a collage on a large sheet of clay placing different groupings over the entire sheet. You can make several projects from one sheet of collaged clay.
- Repeating shapes strengthens the impact of the design.

Border & Pedestal

These elegant pendants are defined by the play on simulated texture and the depth that the simple border provides. The oval shape and texture of the pearls is reflective of the stamens in the stamped floral image. The instructions for the pendants are identical but the shape and the way they are suspended is different.

MATERIALS: Pearl Premo clay shaded with Gray • Black, Warm Gray (scrap mixed together) and Maroon Premo clay (refer to color mixing on page 32) • *Magenta* floral rubber stamp • Colorbox Metallix Extra Peacock Gold pigment ink • Craf-T Mini Metallic paint pots • Classic Shapelets template • Maroon combination fiber strands by Laura Liska Designs • Antique abalone button • 60" strand of freshwater pearls • Thread • Needle • Craft knife • Two rubber bands • Masking tape • Crafter's Pick Ultimate glue

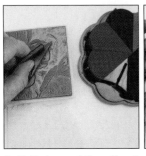    

1. Roll sheet of Gray Pearl clay at #5. **2.** Stamp with floral stamp using pigment ink. **3.** Position square template over stamens in stamped image. **4.** Cut out shape and stack on Black. The next layer is ³⁄₁₆" thick Maroon. Cut a border about ¼" from framed image. **5.** Apply highlight of Metallic Platinum pigment to borders. Bake following manufacturer's instructions.

   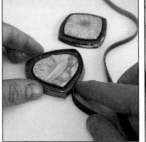 

6. Roll Black and Warm Gray 3" x 6" sheets of clay at #5 setting. Sandwich sheets together. **7.** Run stacked sheets through noodle slicer on pasta machine. **8.** Coat edges with Crafter's Pick glue. **9.** Wrap clay noodle strip around pendant with edges flush at back for raised frame. Smooth seam. **10.** Cut 2" square of Warm Gray and curl over handle of craft knife to make tunnel to hold fibers. Trim to fit on back of pendant and glue in place. Bake and let cool.

11. Cut 60" pieces of fibers. Place pearls and fibers side by side and secure ends with a rubber bands. Tape one end down to anchor, twist cords continuously in one direction. When taut, place finger at mid point and allow cords to twist onto themselves. Rubber band ends. Determine necklace length and trim one end. **12.** Attach button 2" from cut end of cords with thread. **13.** Thread loop end through tunnel on pendant and button necklace.

Pendants

MATERIALS: Pearl Premo clay shaded with Gray • Black, Warm Gray (scrap mixed together) and Maroon Premo clay (refer to color mixing on page 32) • *Magenta* floral rubber stamp • Colorbox Metallix Extra Peacock Gold pigment ink • Craf-T Mini Metallic paint pots • Sterling Silver cord necklace • 2" of 16 gauge Sterling Silver wire • Solid Sterling Silver ring • Leaf Shapelets template • Craft knife • Crafter's Pick Ultimate glue

1. Roll sheet of Gray Pearl clay at #5 setting. Stamp with floral stamp using pigment ink. Position leaf template over blossom in stamped image. Cut out shape.

2. Stack shape on Black. The next layer is ³⁄₁₆" thick Maroon. Cut a border about ¼" from framed image.
3. Apply highlight of Platinum metallic pigment to borders of pendant. Bake pendant.

4. For Silver loop, bend wire over ³⁄₈" diameter pen handle. Cut ends even. **5.** Drill 2 holes centered on top of baked pendant to match width of loop.

 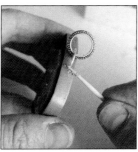

6. Place loop through ring. Dab holes with glue and insert loop into holes. **7.** Fill gaps in holes with Gray clay and rebake. Let cool and add necklace.

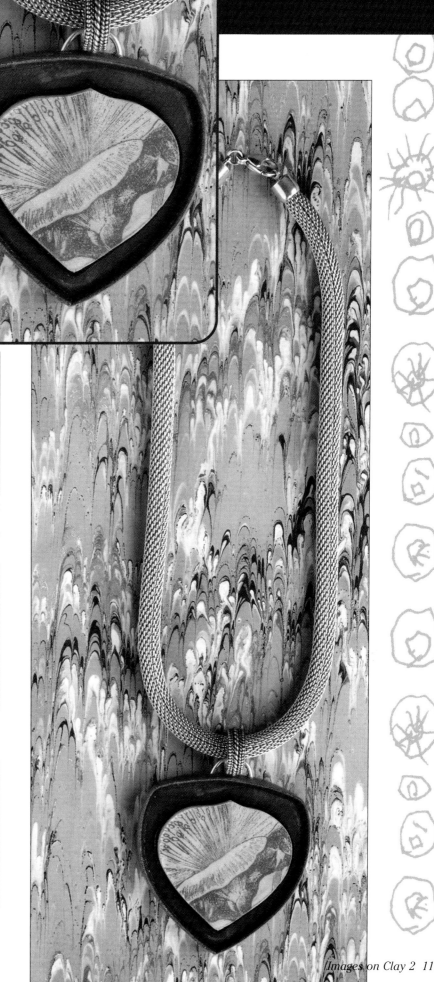

Green Diamond

This project shows varying borders and sequences that are most effective.

MATERIALS: Premo Metallic Gold, Pearl Green clay • Premo Pearl, Premo Black and Orange-Red clay (see page 32 for color mixing) • Triangle transfer • Mulberry paper • Crafter's Pick Ultimate glue • Toner Black stretch cord or Black elastic cord • Black button • Scissors

1. Mix Green clay and roll 1/32" thick sheet at #5. Copy 3 images of triangle and place on clay. Make an extra image in case one doesn't transfer.

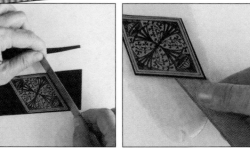 

  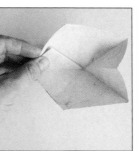  

2. Remove paper. **3.** Trim edges with straight blade. **4.** Place diamond on thin layer rolled at #5 or #6 setting. Trim just beyond first layer for stacked and framed border. The first layer is usually Black for dynamic contrast. In subtler color schemes, Black can be toned down to Gray, Brown or Reddish Black. **5.** Place trimmed piece on another sheet of contrasting color clay. Use blade as a tool to move pieces. This helps keep edges straight and prevents smearing of transfer image. **6.** Stack and trim 2 more layers. The Red layer adds contrast.

7. The Red shows how another color can enliven a project. The final layer is Black to unify composition. **8.** Place diamond on a sheet of paper. Cut paper to accommodate space between panels. **9 & 10.** Make folds to midpoint so the book will tuck and close. **11.** Trim edges.

12. The second style book uses paper to hinge panels. **13.** Glue paper to book panels. You may need to trim paper from edges as it frequently shifts a bit during final folding. **14 & 15.** Closure for book is button on a stretchy cord. Cut cord to wrap twice around book. Thread button and knot cord ends. **16.** Loop button clasp around book as shown and tighten. Trim cord as needed.

Ribbon Journals

MATERIALS: Premo Pearl, Gold and Black clay • 5½" x 6" and 5½" square journals • Rubber stamps (*Magenta* alphabet, *Limited Edition* script, *Hanko Designs* texture swirl) • Imprintz Gold metallic pigment ink • Colorbox Maroon ink • 9" pieces of wide decorative ribbon • Leaf template • Double stick tape • Crafter's Pick Ultimate glue

1. Roll ¹/₁₆" thick strip of Beige clay (Gold and Pearl with a touch of Black) on #3 setting. Dampen Premo clay with water to act as a release agent. Press texture stamp into clay.

2. Use template to cut out 3 leaves. These should be in a row with enough space between to cut outer portion of shape into squares. **3.** Pull out leaves and trim remaining portions into 2" squares. Leave enough room around edge so shape has some border.

These projects use both the positive and the negative of the shape. The texture adds interest to the design. The sequence of the two or three designs in a row also balances and repeats the focal points.

    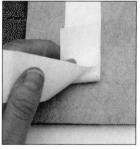

4. Ink and stamp alphabet image on a thin Pearl sheet rolled at #5 setting. **5.** Cut letters into blocks, stack on Black clay. Trim close to edge to create a stacked border. Place initials in center of each leaf. Use Black stacked border to outline shape. For squares, roll thin sheet of Pearl at #5. Stamp script image in Gold pigment ink. Place cut out leaf shape on stamped sheet, trim edges. The script will show through opening. Bake clay pieces. **6 & 7.** Stamp design or script on spine of book. Use a sheet of paper to mask portion of book you do not wish to stamp. **8.** Measure and add ribbon to vertical length of books with double-stick tape. Cut to size. Peel one side of paper and stick on book.

9. Peel off paper and press ribbon into exposed glue. **10.** Tuck and glue ends of ribbon inside cover. **11.** Glue embellishments to top. **12.** You can add more layers of ribbons to enhance design. **13.** Glue baked leaves in a vertical row on ribbons. Place one piece of ribbon inside book for bookmark.

Ancient Image

These images have been embedded in a layer of translucent clay. This enables the image to be handled while shaping the bead. Have fun!

MATERIALS: White and Translucent Premo clay • Photocopy image • *Limited Edition* Asian symbols rubber stamps • Imprintz Gold pigment ink • 2 Bali-type 18mm Sterling Silver bead caps • 2 Gold 10mm bead caps • 4" Gold eye pins • 2 Gold/Pearl 3-strand clasps • Freshwater pearls (six 24" strands, six 7½" strands) • 12 Gold jump rings • White beading thread • Beading needle • Round-nose pliers • Needle tool • Wire rod

INSTRUCTIONS: Make clay bead referring to photos. String pearls to lengths indicated leaving 4" tails. Tie a jump ring to each end of 2 pearl strands. Attach 24" strands to holes in both pieces of one clasp. Attach Pearl piece on second clasp to eye pin at bottom of clay bead and other clasp piece to one end of 7" strands. Attach other ends of strands to eye pin in bead. Join clasps to make necklace.

2. Roll Translucent clay sheet through pasta machine at #4 then at #7. As clay emerges, pull gently. This also helps to prevent ripples or ribbons in clay sheet. Place it evenly on image trying not to trap any air bubbles. This embeds transfer so you can touch it. **3.** Secure layers by rolling brayer over image. Trim the piece.

5. Wrap the core with the prepared transfer. **6.** To wrap the bead with the transfer, slice one edge bluntly and wrap until the ends start to overlap.

 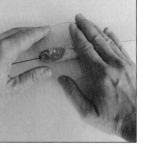

8. Smooth seam. Roll bead to even and smooth surface. At the same time, you can shape bead and taper ends. **9.** Create blimp, sausage or cigar shape, but remember the image will stretch also. Alternate directions as you roll so face does not twist. Slice ends so they are blunt. **10.** Place end cap over top and bottom of bead. **11.** Pierce hole through bead with needle tool and suspend on a wire rod between edges of a pan for baking. **12.** Roll bead after it is on rod to even shape. Bake at 265°F for 25 minutes. Cool. Translucent clay will darken if oven is too hot.

Beads

1. Transfer photocopy to White clay sheet rolled at #5 setting. Remove paper. Stamp Asian characters and icons with Gold ink.

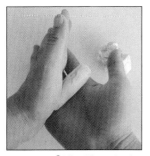

4. Make a ⅜" x 3" snake for a bead core by rolling in palms of hands. Continue to step 5.

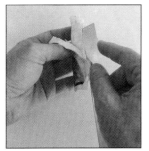

7. Pull overlap back and you will see a slight impression on inside of overlapped clay. Slice along this line to match slices exactly.

13. Insert an eye pin in the bead, make a loop in the straight end and attach the necklace and clasp.

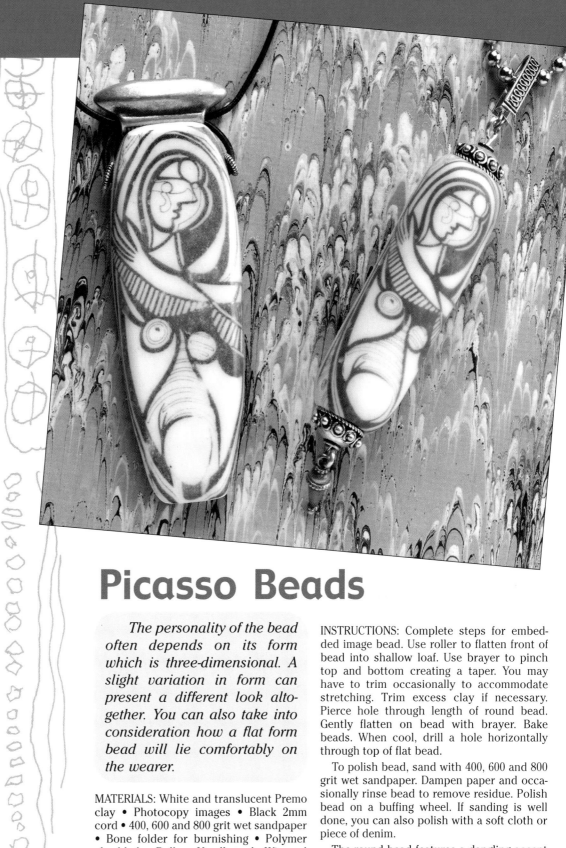

Picasso Beads

The personality of the bead often depends on its form which is three-dimensional. A slight variation in form can present a different look altogether. You can also take into consideration how a flat form bead will lie comfortably on the wearer.

MATERIALS: White and translucent Premo clay • Photocopy images • Black 2mm cord • 400, 600 and 800 grit wet sandpaper • Bone folder for burnishing • Polymer clay blade • Roller • Needle tool • Wire rod • Craft drill • Polishing wheel or cloth

FLAT BEAD MATERIALS: 2mm Black cord • 30mm long Silver bead • 2 Silver 6mm rondelles

ROUND BEAD MATERIALS: Silver ball chain • 2 Silver 18mm bead caps • 4" Silver eye pin • 5mm x 20mm Silver bail • Silver charm

INSTRUCTIONS: Complete steps for embedded image bead. Use roller to flatten front of bead into shallow loaf. Use brayer to pinch top and bottom creating a taper. You may have to trim occasionally to accommodate stretching. Trim excess clay if necessary. Pierce hole through length of round bead. Gently flatten on bead with brayer. Bake beads. When cool, drill a hole horizontally through top of flat bead.

To polish bead, sand with 400, 600 and 800 grit wet sandpaper. Dampen paper and occasionally rinse bead to remove residue. Polish bead on a buffing wheel. If sanding is well done, you can also polish with a soft cloth or piece of denim.

The round bead features a dangling accent and is held by an eye pin. The flat bead is strung with a leather cord that has been double crossed though a long bead. To knot cord with a hangman's knot, cross cords at ends and loop one end back toward itself. Then wrap around other cord and loop. When length runs out, thread end through loop. Pull cord that began the wrap tight. Repeat on end of other cord.

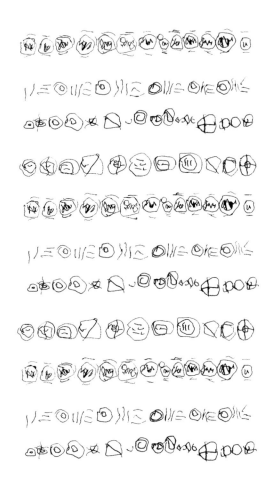
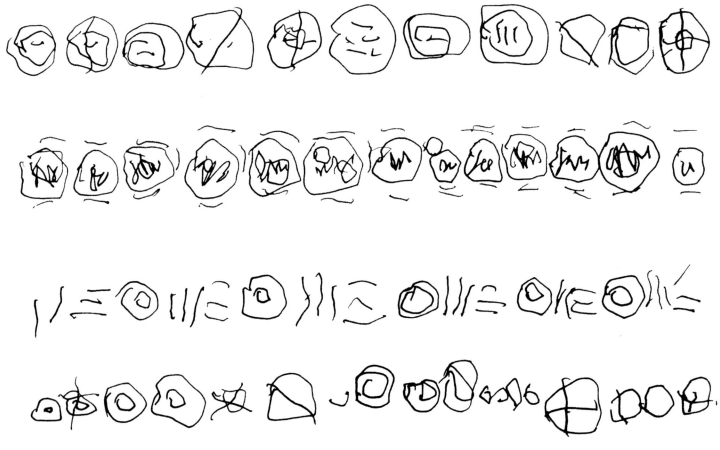

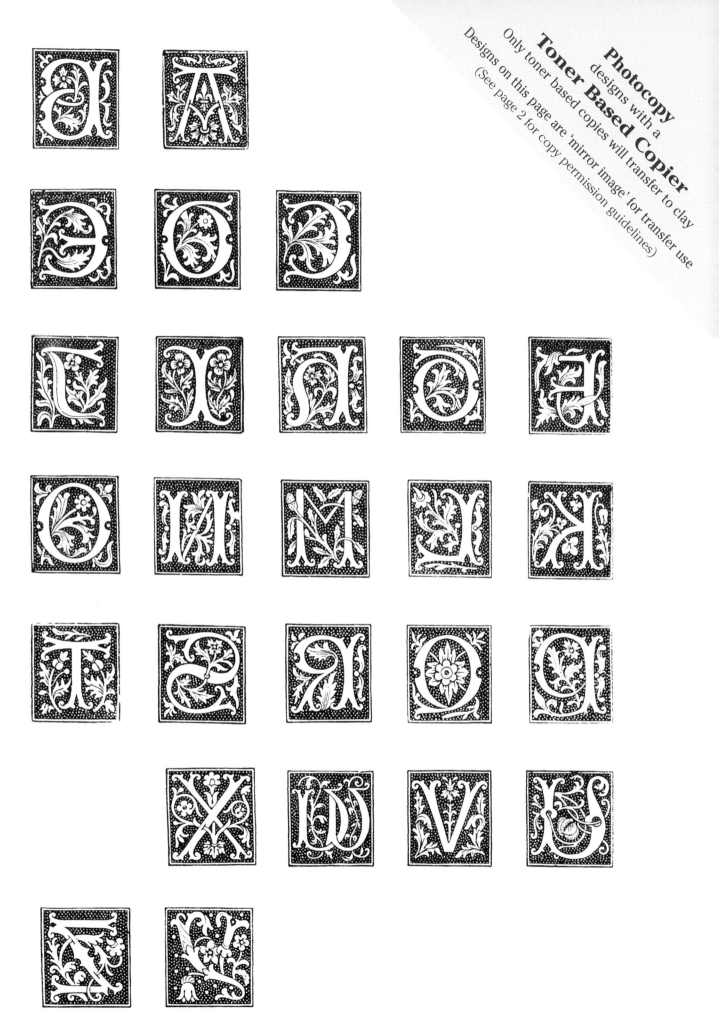

Photocopy
designs with a
Toner Based Copier
Only toner based copies will transfer to clay
Designs on this page are 'mirror image' for transfer use
(See page 2 for copy permission guidelines)

Images on Clay 2 17

Photocopy
designs with a
Toner Based Copier
Only toner based copies will transfer to clay
Designs on this page are 'mirror image' for transfer use
(See page 2 for copy permission guidelines)

Images on Clay 2 19

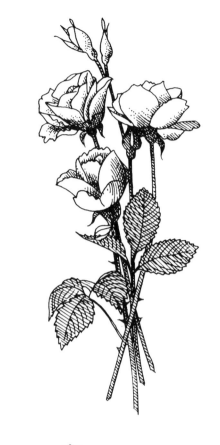

FIG. XXXI.—Œnothera biennis : 1, vertical section of a flower ; 2, 3, stamens ;
4, pollen grains ; 5, the 4 stigmas on 1 style ; 6, a capsule, 4-valved ; 7,—4-celled ;
8, a seed ; 9, seed dissected ; 10, the 2-lobed embryo.

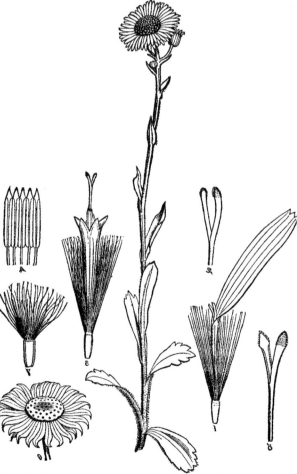

FIG. XXXVI.—Erigeron bellidifolium: 1, a ray floret; 2, its style and stigmas; 3, a disk
...st: 4, its stamens; 5, its pistil; 6, receptacle and involucre; 7, ripe fruit and pappus.

The Involucre consists of many nearly equal scales,
...en, linear, pointed, and all in one row, not imbricated (6).
...e receptacle (6) is flat, naked (no chaff among the florets),

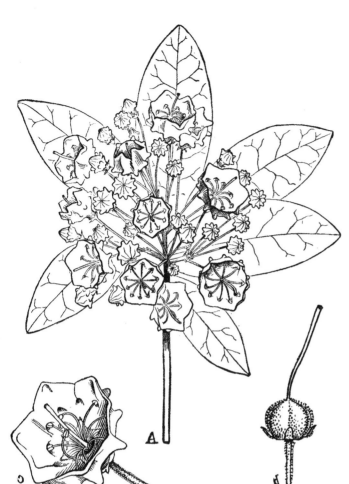

Fig. XLI.—Kalmia latifolia: c, a flower natural size; b, a growing ovary, with its style.

tical, acute at each end, supported on short petioles. Its
flowers are in large terminal corymbs, viscid-pubescent,
white varying to rose-color.

The other species are shrublets 1–3 feet in height. The

Fig. XXX.—Robinia Pseudacacia: 1, the calyx, stamens and pistil, or the flower
minus the corolla; 2, the stamens displayed; 3, the pistil with ovary dissected; 4,
the fruit.

122

Images on Clay 2 21

Macaroni Beads

A bead form can also be defined by the size of the hole through the bead. If beads have a curved tube shape, the form allows a bracelet to fit around the wrist.

1. Size, photocopy and transfer drawings to White sheets of clay.

MATERIALS: White and Translucent Premo clay • Kid's drawings • 4 Pale Blue 12mm resin cylinder beads • 16 Silver bead caps • Stretch memory elastic • Nested brass cylinder tubes for making holes • Optional: 16 gauge Sterling Silver wire and Sterling Silver S hook

4. Cut edges to match & smooth seams. Bake beads on wire rods suspended in a box.

7. Begin loop of eye pin, inserting wire in center of pliers, turn away from body as you wrap using the widest area of pliers.

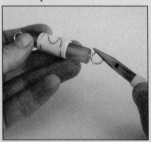

10. Insert round-nose pliers and bring loop back into place at top of straight wire.

1. The designs that inspired this project were drawn by very young children on strips of paper. The drawings were then assembled to make a complete image. **2.** Transfer and embed images. **3.** Wrap snake of clay as in making a long image embedded bead. See page 14.

 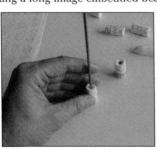 

4. Trim and smooth bead seams. Cut into sections. **5.** Punch hole through bead with a hollow brass tube. **6.** You will be extruding some clay from center of bead.

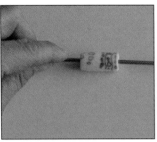   

7. Use a smaller diameter tube to clear any remaining clay in bead. On a flat surface, roll the bead smooth with tube inserted. The pressure of tube against the wall of the bead will widen hole. **8.** Bend bead slightly. Bake. **9.** When cool, string with bead end caps and elastic. Hide the knotted elastic inside one bead. **10.** Another way to finish bracelet is to make an eye on one end of 6" of 16 gauge Sterling Silver wire. Thread beads and bead caps. Make another eye and attach S hook to close bracelet.

2. Embed transferred designs in Translucent clay.
3. Cut designs into squares or strips, large enough to wrap around resin beads. Vary widths.

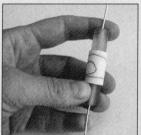

5. Cut length of Sterling Silver wire 2" longer than bead making sure ends are flush cut. 6. Hold finger over end of wire while cutting.

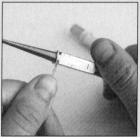
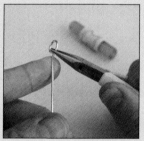

8. Reposition wire in the pliers and continue turning until loop is complete. 9. Bend loop back at neck using chain-nose pliers.

11. Make another loop on the open end and trim any excess wire. 12. Make the rings to connect the necklace together by wrapping wire around a pen, dowel stick or jewelry mandrel. Slip rings off in a continuous spiral.

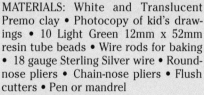

MATERIALS: White and Translucent Premo clay • Photocopy of kid's drawings • 10 Light Green 12mm x 52mm resin tube beads • Wire rods for baking • 18 gauge Sterling Silver wire • Round-nose pliers • Chain-nose pliers • Flush cutters • Pen or mandrel

This project came from two inspirations. First, I wanted to make a necklace for a teacher from strips of patterns drawn by very young children. Second, I wanted to use the beautiful sheer resin beads. The sheer quality of the beads in contrast to the opaque clay wrap creates texture as well as a spatial relationship.

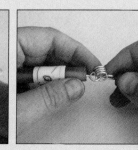

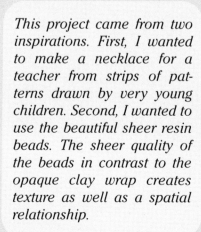

13. Cut rings apart every 3 full turns using flush edge of cutters. Recut one end of each ring to make both ends flush. 14. Thread wire through both loops of 2 adjacent beads, turn until rings are inside loops. 15. Pinch wires together with chain-nose pliers springing tension until rings are taut.

Half Cylinder Beads

Half cylinder beads make a great bracelet. The core of the bead is scrap from previous transfer projects.

MATERIALS: Leftover portions or strips of embedded images • Scrap clay for bead core • 18mm half cylinder resin beads with 2 holes • Needle tool • Craft drill • Elastic or Miracle stretch cord

 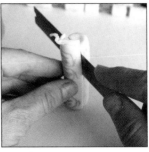 

1. Roll a snake of scrap clay about ¾" diameter. Place embedded image strips over top curve of scrap snake. **2.** Cut snake into small portions that can stand upright and slice vertically. **3.** Size decorated side of half cylinder to match size of accent beads by stretch or pushing.

 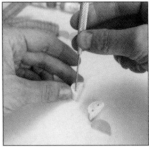 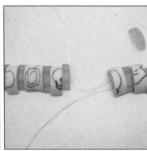

4. Slice half cylinder into chunks in a variety of widths. **5.** Drill 2 holes evenly spaced through bead with needle tool. These holes should match holes in acrylic beads. **6.** Bake. String clay beads alternating with resin beads on elastic cord. Widen holes in one of the beads to hide knot.

Banded Bracelets

 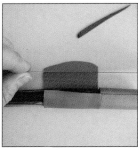 

1. Choose a selection of solid color clays. Use a bright accent color with Grays and Beiges. **2.** Roll ⅜" x 8" snake of scrap clay for core of bracelet. Cover snake with thin sheets of colored clay. Trim sheets so seam does not overlap. **3.** Trim edges of wrapped clay so next color wrap is flush with first color wrap.

  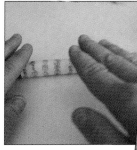

4. Wrap cut sheet of embedded transfer design around remainder of bracelet. Trim to fit with no overlap. **5.** Smooth seams together with bone burnisher. **6.** Roll entire bracelet smooth.

  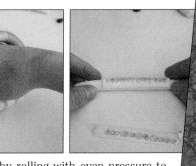

7. Measure snake around wrist and size by rolling with even pressure to stretch or trim to make shorter. Bring bracelet ends together. Cut ends blunt and press together. Add Silver ring if desired. **8.** Smooth connecting seam by rocking back and forth on a flat work surface. Slip gently over the wrist again to make sure it fits. **9.** Roll ⅜" diameter snake of clay and cover with strip of image clay. Slice off top portion of curved image.

 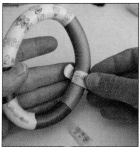 

10. Place slice on finger to shape band. **11.** Choose a seam you wish to hide or support. Cut desired length of image band and wrap around seam. Trim and smooth ends together. **12.** Bake bracelet on fiberfill to support variations in shape.

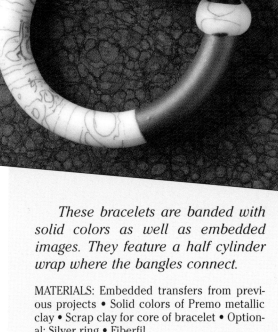

These bracelets are banded with solid colors as well as embedded images. They feature a half cylinder wrap where the bangles connect.

MATERIALS: Embedded transfers from previous projects • Solid colors of Premo metallic clay • Scrap clay for core of bracelet • Optional: Silver ring • Fiberfil

Transferred Panel Candleholder

MATERIALS: Photocopies of child's drawings • White and Translucent Premo clay • Premo Gold blended with Premo Black to make Bronze clay • Craft drill • Raffia • Template made from plastic canvas for base panel • Wrought iron candleholder with sections suitable for panels

1. Measure size of panel needed to fit candleholder. Make template from plastic canvas. Condition and roll 3 White $3/32$" thick and 3 Bronze $1/8$" thick flat sheets. Transfer drawings to White panels. Embed image in very thin Translucent clay sheets.

2. Slice any air pockets that may be trapped by inserting clay blade at an angle and releasing trapped air.
3. Trim panel using template.

4. Press image panel on Bronze panel. Repeat for each panel needed. **5.** Trim outer edges of Bronze panels. Bake panels.

6. Drill holes evenly spaced along sides of each panel.
7. Thread raffia through holes and around legs of candleholder to secure panels.

Your child's drawings will give this unique candleholder personalized charm and turn it into a true 'work of art'.

1. Tint Pearl clay by adding a tiny bit of Gold to a large portion of Pearl.

2. Roll a sheet of tinted Pearl. Use glass from the frame to mark the size of the clay panel.

3. Transfer image to a sheet of clay.

4. Stamp over image with Asian assorted characters using Gold ink.

5. Stamp with Red ink. Bake piece. Let cool and insert in frame with glass behind the clay image.

Transfer Portrait Painting

MATERIALS: Pearl and Gold Premo clay • Photocopy of an Asian portrait image • *Limited Edition* small Asian character rubber stamps • Red Inkredible heat set pigment ink • Imprints Metallic Gold pigment ink • Frame with wrought iron stand

If you begin with an elegant image, it takes only a few accents and strategic placement to make an attractive composition. The frame unifies the piece. The background clay is tinted a very light, soft color to further enhance the picture. Bright White would be too bold and Translucent would be too Yellow unless it were backed by White. These small decisions make all the difference. Although the composition is simple, each detail is carefully planned. This project exemplifies the common phrase, 'less is more'.

Basic Mokume Stacks for Surface Designs

Mokume Gane is a Japanese layering technique where sheets of a material are assembled and the horizontal plane of the stack is altered. When the stack is sliced on the horizontal plane after alteration, it reveals the distortion in each level creating unpredictable lines, ripples, waves and outlines. Even a slight variation in depth will produce a different sequence of color. Mokume sheets are perfect for embellishing and framing abstract design elements. Important elements in Mokume Gane are choice of color, contrasting position of color, thinness of layers and deepness of impressions or distortions. If you are impressing a rubber stamp to alter the stacked clay, the layers should be thin and the cut of the stamp should be deep.

 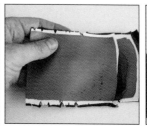  

1. Prepare thin sheets at #6 setting of each of color. Layer stack in the following order to get some blending and some contrast: Blue-Black, Maroon, White, Bronze and Teal. You can make one stack with different color combinations on each side of this stack. **2.** When clay is assembled, run the stack through pasta machine at #2 setting. This helps release air bubbles that may have been trapped and smooth stack. **3.** Cut sheet in half and stack. Do not match the sides, but place one on top of another. When stacked, run through pasta machine again at #2 setting. This thins layers even more. Place results on a sheet of Translucent clay rolled at #4 setting. This will serve as a base for your work. **4.** The next step is to alter layers by pushing objects into stack. Dampen Premo clay so articles will not stick. Use items such as furniture floor guards, child's building toys, combs, pasta wheels and wallpaper scrapers. **5.** These articles create impressions that are classic patterns such as circles, broken lines and dots. They are pleasing to the eye because they are familiar and have rhythm.

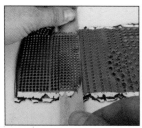    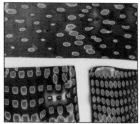

6. Place stack on a surface where it will not slide around. It is best if stack is anchored to a tacky surface such as a Formica top or an acrylic sheet. Slice thin layers across top of stack horizontally using tissue blade. Cut as many layers as possible. This might take some practice before you are comfortable handling the blade. **7, 8 & 9.** Colors and patterns will emerge. **10.** Run some of the surface design through pasta machine to stretch for another interesting effect.

Stamped Mokume Stacks

1. Create a subtle color palette that has some contrast in value from light to dark. **2.** Assemble thin layers and run through pasta machine to thin. Dampen sheet with water and press stamps into stack. **3.** Slice through layers. Since you are trying to salvage outline of the stamp, slice small portions at a time. **4.** Place scraps on an additional sheet set aside for this purpose. **5.** Run caught scrap sheet through the pasta machine to even out surface. All surface design sheets you have made will be utilized in other projects.

Mokume Transfer Bracelets

Choose 5 colors including a very dark, almost Black and a very light almost White. The Premo clay colors in this project are based on choices from the color wheel on pages 32 and 33.

Deep Blue Black = ½ Blue Pearl + ½ Black
Maroon = ¼ Copper + ¾ Blue Pearl
Bronze = ½ Gold + ½ Black
White Pearl = ¼ White + ¾ Pearl
Neutral Gray = ½ Gold + ½ Silver which serves as complete neutral.

Neutral Gray may seem like a boring color but it gives a balance to intense colors and mellows them so they won't be so competitive next to each other. When colors are vying for attention, it is good for them to be noticed but they should not compete with one another.

VERY IMPORTANT NOTE: It is an excellent practice to make a tiny test stack of assorted colors before you assemble mounds of clay to be sure you are happy with the layered colors. Combinations that contain too many colors will be muddy. It is best to limit your colors to one side of the color wheel at a time.

In previous projects you have learned the skills to make this bracelet. This is another way to combine design elements and create a new look.

MATERIALS: Sheets of Mokume stack surface design • Embedded transfer of Picasso Modern art with Translucent overlay • Core of scrap clay in colors used for the stack • Small ball chain • Sterling bands • Super glue

1. Roll ⅜" diameter snake for core of bracelet. Encase bracelet in thin sheet of solid color. Roll smooth. Place a sheet of embedded image on bracelet. **2.** Prepare thin patches of Mokume slices. **3.** Place trimmed patches and strips of Mokume on bracelet. **4.** When everything is placed, roll smooth. **5.** A trick I learned from Carol Shelton is to roll the snake under a sheet of acrylic to even it out and make it ultra smooth.

  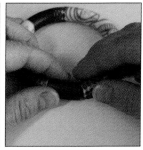  

6. Cut ends blunt. **7.** Optional: Slip a Sterling Silver band on ends and connect bracelet. This is a little tricky and usually the bracelet must be secured again with glue after baking. Or just slip band over bracelet. **8.** Connect and smooth ends. **9.** Wrap ball chain around the connection in bracelet. Bake bracelet. **10.** When cool, pull ball chain back slightly and glue permanently into place with super glue.

Banded & Capped Beads

These beads all incorporate Mokume Gane and a band of embedded transferred drawings. The beads are capped in different styles. This illustrates how important it is to finish the hole of the bead and what a difference this design decision will make in the final presentation of the bead. The stringing of the necklace will also create a different look including asymmetrical compositions. The purchased beads should complement the shape and color of the handmade beads.

MATERIALS: Transferred drawings embedded in Translucent clay • Surface design of Mokume Gane • Scrap clay for core of bead • Sterling Silver beads • Pearls • E beads • Coral beads • Bone beads • Sterling Silver clasps • Soft flex wire • Crimp beads • ¾" round Kemper punch • Chain-nose pliers • Round-nose pliers • Needle tool • Wire rod • Acrylic sheet

INSTRUCTIONS: Roll snake of Mokume and embed images very straight by rolling bead under a piece of acrylic. Slice beads into sections. Use a rolling motion as you slice downward to keep ends blunt and bead round.

Roll a flat sheet of Black clay at #4 setting. Punch ¾" circles from the clay. Center bead on Black circle and press firmly to attach circle to bead. Lift the bead by sliding blade under circle. Press other end on another circle and lift. Pierce hole though bead with needle tool. String beads on wire rod and suspend between 2 supports while baking.

Rounded Black Caps

INSTRUCTIONS: Follow directions for straight circle caps, but make beads slightly smaller in diameter and taper ends of beads slightly. Smooth circles over ends and pierce holes.

Beads with Glass Bead Finish

INSTRUCTIONS: Roll ¾" x 8" snake from scraps of solid color clay. Cover snake with scraps from Mokume stack. Embed transfer in Translucent clay. In this project modern freehand drawings are used. Cut strips of transfer clay. Wrap strips around snake leaving about 1" between strips. Roll snake smooth so wrapped design sinks into surface. Slice snake into 1" sections and roll into ovals. Pinch and taper ends while you roll beads between palms of your hands. Pierce with a needle tool and place bead caps on ends. String beads on a straight wire rod and suspend between 2 supports while baking.

Finishing Necklaces & Bracelets

String on Soft Flex wire, leather or waxed linen that will not cut into clay. Use small spacers between larger beads to hide the cord as it curves. To finish clasp, thread cord through crimp bead, then through loop attached to clasp and double it back through crimp. Pinch crimp and cut excess wire so tail of cords can be tucked into beads. If there is no clasp, just a continuous cord, insert ends through crimp from both directions, pinch crimp, cut excess cord and tuck ends of cord into beads.

Bead Earrings

The small details are what define the personality of earrings. Considerations such as size, weight and balance are crucial. The cap on a bead can make it look modern or ancient. Notice these details and construction when you are shopping and anywhere jewelry is displayed. In many cases, a head pin with a metal ball or decorative detail at one end is used instead of an eye pin.

MATERIALS: 2 small Mokume Gane beads • 4 small Sterling Silver bead end caps • 2 Sterling Silver fish hook ear wires with ball and loop ends • 2 Ball end head pins • Round-nose pliers • Chain-nose pliers

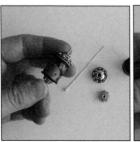  

1. Insert head pin into caps and beads. **2.** Make loop at top of head pin. The loop should be made near tip of pliers for small opening so hole is relatively small. **3.** Open loop on ear wires and attach beads. NOTE: You can lengthen earrings or add movement by inserting additional jump rings between ear wires and hanging beads.

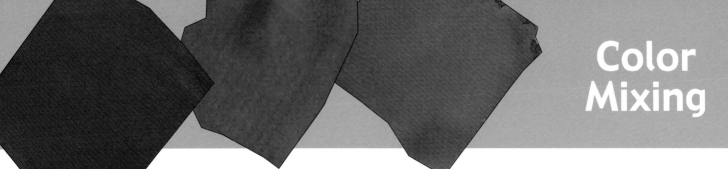

Color Mixing

The first and foremost thing a person needs to understand about design is color. Especially in clay, if you get the color in harmony, then your piece has appeal. Clay is a most excellent medium to understand color and color mixing because you can repeatedly measure exact proportions to duplicate a color or change it slightly. You can also watch the color as it changes in your hands and experience the potential for other proportions as you mix. Clay also allows you to experiment by laying one color over another like a veil and shading one color into another to make a blend.

There are three artists who have greatly enhanced my understanding of color. They are Maggie Maggio, Judith Skinner and Lindley Huanani. Lindley and Maggie have presented a method for mixing color that is flawless and reveals the understanding behind the compatibility of color. It also is transferable to any medium that can be measured like dyes and paints.

Polymer clay is just like paint, you can mix two or more hues to get another color. Of course there are many beautiful combinations along the way. To mix the color, make two sheets and run them through the pasta machine together. Split the clay in half, stack and run it through again. Keep doing this until the color is completely blended.

To make an exact color or repeat a color, use this ingenious color chart developed by Maggie Maggio as a reference. This is an invaluable and accurate way to determine exact color proportions and achieve the same colors repeatedly. It is also a way to choose colors that will be harmonious with each other because they are formulated with the same primaries.

The primary colors are Red, Yellow and Blue. Secondary colors are combinations of the primaries, Orange, Green and Purple. You can use any Red, Yellow and Blue to make a hue circle. The results will vary depending on how pure and saturated the pigments are.

This system does not teach color theory; it teaches accurate mixing of the primaries. Throughout the book, I have mainly used metallic and pearl primary colors plus Black, White, Pearl and Translucent. The primaries for this mixing chart, a string of beads, are Premo Metallic Gold, Metallic Copper, Pearl Blue. Please note that the hue circle would be very different if I chose Pearl Red instead of Metallic Copper.

This system also works for mixing secondary colors and any tints, adding White, or shades, adding Black. We will not go into all the mixing options. The basic system applies to all combinations of color. You are encouraged to make several of your favorite combinations for reference and accurate color duplication. Taking the guesswork out of mixing color saves time and clay! I wish to thank Maggie for her willingness to share this incredible system for the benefit of all of us who wish to create with polymer clay.

   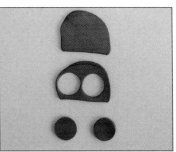

1. Pick one Yellow, one Blue and one Red. These are the 3 primaries. **2.** Flatten each of these clays into sheets on thickest setting on pasta machine. Use same setting throughout this project to maintain consistency and accuracy. Make sure colors are pure, even a small speck can alter a hue. Prepare one sheet each and punch 10 circles of each color. The punch cuts even amounts out of the clay. Disk punch cutters by Kemper are excellent, but any consistent shape will do. **3.** To start hue circle, add 2 punched circles of Blue and 2 circles of Gold, blend thoroughly. This color represents exactly ½ Blue and ½ Gold which is Green. **4.** This will be a midpoint at which we will work back to the pure hue. Roll this combination into a sheet and punch out 2 circles.

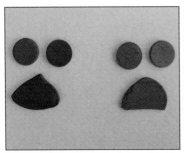 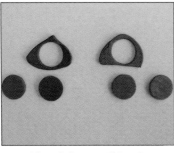 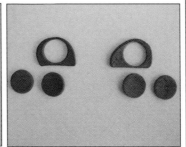 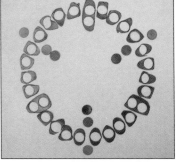

10, 11 & 12. Eventually Green will be so diluted that it will be close to original hues, Blue or Gold. **13.** The finished cut out circles arranged as the process is executed look like this. NOTE: I have added a shade, ½ Black and a tint ½ White, to each of the primaries. Add an additional circle of color to each of the primaries to make those beads larger and easier to identify.

Color
Necklace

Practice color mixing and combinations while you create this rainbow.

MATERIALS: Premo clay (Metallic Gold, Metallic Copper Pearl Blue) • Kemper punch circle or (or any cut-out tool) • Needle tool

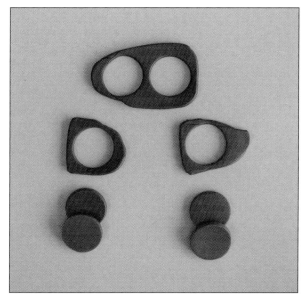

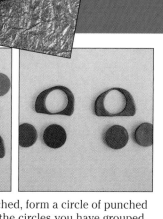

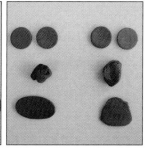  

5. Set aside the remaining Green which becomes the mid point between Blue and Gold. As each portion is punched, form a circle of punched out scraps. You now have 2 Green circles. Add a Blue to one Green and a Gold to the other Green. **6.** Now mix the circles you have grouped. **7.** Flatten mix and punch circles again. Add another Blue and Gold. **8.** Each time a Blue or Gold circle is added, the Green is diluted and moves closer to the original colors of Gold and Blue. **9.** Continue this process of adding a circle, flattening and punching out a circle and adding more color to the punched circle. The mixing proportions of color will be $1/2 + 1/2$; $1/4 + 3/4$; $7/8 + 1/8$; $1/16 + 15/16$, etc.

 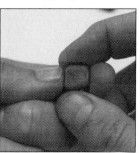 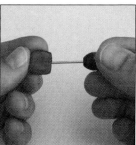 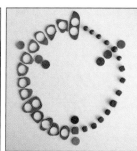 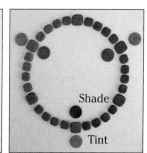

14. Roll each scrap into a ball and flatten. **15.** Pinch flat clay into a square bead. **16.** Pierce hole through bead for stringing. **17.** The hue circle will begin to look like this. **18.** The finished wheel will look like this. Bake beads. Be careful to keep them in order. String beads.

Botanical Translucent Panels

These projects are supposed to be light and airy. Inks are iridescent metallic. This is a big project that covers a lot of space. It is a little scary at first to go big in your art, but once you do, you have opened your creativity to a new realm. These panels can also be used as lamp panel inserts and window hanging collages. Copy plant form sequences or any other series of drawings. I was fascinated by fine line drawings. Depending on the stamps and images chosen, the designs could take on a completely different character.

Hanging Frame

MATERIALS: Polymer clay • Photocopy images • Assorted rubber stamps • Tsukineko Light colored metallic inks • Hanging frame with glass • Cardstock • Clay blade • Pen • Scissors

INSTRUCTIONS: Make transfer panel. Remove glass from frame and cut panel to fit. Bake panel. With clay on outside, insert panel and glass in frame.

MANY THANKS to my friends for their cheerful help and wonderful ideas!
Production Director - Kathy McMillan
Art Department Manager - Jen Tennyson
Graphic Artists - Patty Williams & Marti Wyble
Copy Editors - Wanda J. Little & Colleen Reigh
Photography - David & Donna Thomason